Gold from Norfolk

by

The Pupils of

Snettisham Primary School,

Norfolk

with John Haden

ISBN No: 978.1.906542.95.5
Publishers: Barny Books
             76 Cotgrave Lane, Tollerton, NG32 2HL
             Tel: +44(0)115 937 5147
             www.**barnybooks**.co.uk/

Copies of this book and the others in the Books with Schools and
ARIES series may be obtained from the Publisher or from:

Books with Schools Project
13 St Albans Close, Oakham
Rutland LE15 6EW
Tel: 01572 720428

Contents

Foreword: Metals the Romans used

This is a book about a metal, one of the six metals which the Romans used when they occupied Britain about two thousand years ago. The six metals are gold, silver, copper, lead, tin and iron. We have been using these metals ever since and many others which the Romans did not know.

All metals are elements and scientists have given our six metals symbols which come from the Latin names which the Romans gave them: Au from Aurum, Ag from Argentum, Cu from Cuprum, Pb from Plumbum, Sn from Stannum and Fe from Ferrum. Not all metals have Latin names; zinc and nickel for example, which have symbols: Zn and Ni.

This book is the first to be written with schools about metals the Romans used. Our books will be about people as much as about metals, how towns and villages grew up around the places where the metals were found, or where rocks containing the metals were dug out of the ground. They are also about how those communities suffered when things went wrong. When, for example, they could no longer produce the metal which they had come to depend on cheaply enough to sell to others.

Our six metals share some properties. They are all conductors of heat, but some are much better conductors than others so we find them very useful for making pans to cook our food. They are also all conductors of electricity and some are especially good, so we used them for electrical wiring. Some are especially easy to beat out flat into a thin sheet or to stretch into a thin wire - they are said to be malleable and ductile.

Some of them are very shiny – they are lustrous. Some stay shiny even when buried in the earth. Others soon lose their shiny surface and even fall into pieces if they are not kept away from air and water - they corrode.

Metals can be mixed together to form what we call alloys. Copper and tin make a hard strong alloy called bronze. You may have heard of the Bronze Age. Iron is the most useful metal in our list, and also the most common. It was used by people in England from the start of the time we call the Iron Age. Iron can also be made into a magnet which will attract other pieces of iron, but none of the other five in our list has this property of magnetism.

We are all encouraged not to waste metals, but to recycle them. That's because we all live on a beautiful blue spaceship, Planet Earth, which is big enough to take all 7 billion of us humans speeding through space on our annual journey around our Sun. Major Tim Peake, the British astronaut who was in space in orbit around the Earth when we were writing this book, could see that Blue Planet from the port-hole of his Space Station. He and the other astronauts all had to take the things they needed with them when they blasted off from the Earth. You cannot pop out to the corner shop to get a loaf of bread when you are in space!

Fortunately, on our space ship, we have all the things we need, oxygen to breathe, water to drink and food to eat. We have sunshine to keep us warm and soil in which to grow our food. We share our spaceship with an amazing collection of animals, birds and fishes, plants and trees and many other living things, some even too small to be seen.

Our books are not just written for schools, although we hope that schools will find them useful. They are also written for visitors to the places where we live. We hope that you enjoy reading our accounts of the metals the Romans used and hope that you too may be keen to find out more about the places we call home. And don't forget, we have what we need only if we keep re-cycling the metals which we use. When you are on a space-ship, you only have what you take with you!

John Haden

Our space-ship, the beautiful Blue Planet we call Earth,
viewed from Space

1. Snettisham – our Norfolk village

If you are on holiday and you drive north from the port of King's Lynn on the road at first signed to Cromer and then turn off to Hunstanton, you pass a chain of villages, Sandringham, Dersingham, Snettisham and Heacham. Where the great bay of the Wash meets the North Sea, at the North-West corner of Norfolk, you reach 'sunny Hunny', Hunstanton, with its popular beach. On the map of NW Norfolk the four villages you pass all have names ending in '-ham' and the town's name end in '-ton' – why do these places all have '-ham' and '-ton' names?

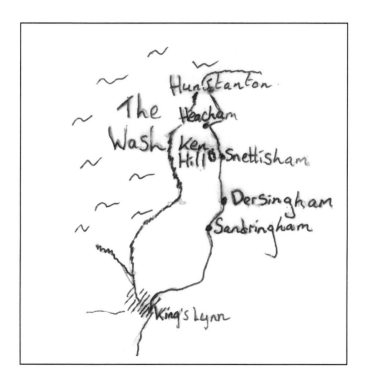

Map of NW Norfolk by Lily W. and Jasmine D.

We thought that a clue to an answer to that question might be on the village sign by the roadside as you drive into Snettisham. This sign shows two tough looking men and an open sailing boat, perhaps a picture of the Anglo-Saxons who came across the North Sea to invade and settle this part of England. After the Romans had left Britain, in the 5th and 6th Century AD, Angles and Saxons invaded England and settled in the east and south of the British Isles. But when we looked at the men on the sign more closely, we saw that one had a pistol in his hand and the other was carrying a lamp and had a swag-bag of goods over his shoulder! So they were not Saxons, but must be smugglers from a later age.

The village sign on the roadside at the south of our village.

But the Anglo-Saxons did invade this part of England. They pushed the original Celtic people we used to call the Ancient Britons west into Wales and Cornwall and settled in what we now know as Norfolk. One gave his name to 'Snaet's place', now Snettisham. Others settled in Heacham, Dersingham, and Sandringham and yet more settled in other NW Norfolk villages, Burnham, Thornham, Bircham, Rudham, Massingham, Congham and Swaffham – all Anglo-Saxon settlements. We still use the word 'hamlet' for a small village or settlement.

On the village sign, alongside the two smugglers and their sailing boat, are two sea-horses for this is a place very near to the East Coast. It is also famous for the sea-birds who follow the tide up out of their muddy feeding grounds in the Wash. Thousands of waders in the summer and thousands of geese in the winter come in to settle on the gravel shore at the RSPB Reserve at Snettisham Beach, waiting for the tide to turn so they can fly back out to feed on the mud and sand banks left by the tide.

Waders coming in from the Wash to settle at High Tide on the RSPB Reserve at Snettisham beach

Famous for Anglo-Saxons, smugglers and sea-birds, but there is another part of Snettisham's rich history shown on the village sign. Across the top is a curved yellow object, which could be a piece of jewelry or an ornament. In fact it is a Torc, the other reason why Snettisham is famous and where gold comes into our story. Torcs are clearly very important to the village because there is a Torc Bookshop, a Torc Motors business at Dersingham and the village newsletter is called the 'Torc of Snettisham'.

Even our school, Snettisham Primary, has a torc
as our school badge.

What exactly is a 'torc'?

A torc is a metal band made in a horseshoe shape which can be worn as a piece of jewelry. They can be big or small, worn on your neck or arms or even like a belt. The smallest ones can be used as ear-rings. The oldest ones come from the Bronze Age, over 1000 years BC.

(by Jack I.)

Torcs were worn by chiefs and kings and their wives by many Celtic tribes in Britain and showed the status of the person wearing the torc. They were worn from the Bronze Age well into the Iron Age and even at the time when the Romans invaded Britain in AD 43. Iron age peoples also believed that their torcs had mystical powers to ward off evil and to protect the wearer. Later, in Roman times, it became more of a decoration or a fashion item.

Snettisham's Great Torc

By far the finest of all the torcs ever found in England is the Great Torc of Snettisham. It was made by twisting 64 threads of gold, each 1.9 mm wide, to form eight separate ropes of metal. These were then twisted around each other to make the horse-shoe shaped torc. The two open ends were then put in moulds so that hollow terminals could be welded onto the ropes. These terminals were made ornamental with embossed ridges and some 'basket-work' decorations. Some people claim that the terminals show the faces of two Celtic people!

The torc is mostly made of gold alloyed with a small amount of silver. It measures 199mm across and weighs just over 2 kg. Norfolk Museum Services expert Dr John Davies said that the Great Torc dated back to the Iceni tribe and could have belonged to an important member of the tribe. Boudica, the Iceni Queen, could have worn similar jewelry.

A report by Dr J D Hill of the British Museum revealed that the torc was made between 200 and 50 BC. They knew this because some coins and other jewelry from that time were found with the torc.

Soon after it was discovered in 1950, it was declared 'treasure trove'. This meant that no-one knew who owned it when it was found hidden in the ground so it was declared to be property of the State. The British Museum was able to buy the torc with the support of the National Art Collections fund and it is now held on display in the British Museum.

(by Mithu B., Olivia D., Jack I., Aimee K. and LeahY.)

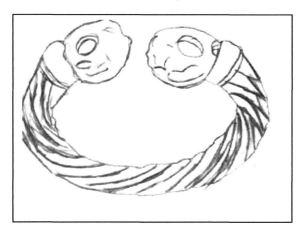

Drawing of the Snettisham Great Torc by Megan C.
(Are those human faces on the terminals?)

Haiku on finding the great torc by Callum E.

Digging up slowly

Never knowing what you're finding

Then, a special torc!

2. Finding the first Gold on Ken Hill

The Great Torc was not the first gold to be found at Snettisham. At the end of World War II, England was running out of food. In spite of rationing, a system which the Government used to control the food supply to families to ensure that everyone had their fair share of what little there was, there was not enough food. Now the War was over, people wanted more. So the call went out to England's farmers to grow more food. Even poor land, land which had been used for non-food crops, was to be ploughed up and brought into cultivation.

To the north and west of Snettisham, the land is poor, just a thin layer of chalky soil lying over the soft brown stone which is called Carstone (sometimes spelled Carrstone). This stone lies under Ken Hill just to the west of Snettisham. If you go futher north to Hunstanton beach at low tide and stand with your back to the sea, you can see the cliff, with brown carstone at the base, a thin layer of red chalk and then a layer of white chalk at the top.

Aerial view of the town of Hunstanton on the Norfolk Coast, with the chalk and carstone cliffs above the beach.

Leah Y. has drawn a diagram of these layers to make them easier to understand:

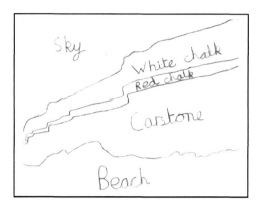

At Hunstanton, the chalk layers are quite thick, with the white chalk just under the top soil, then a thin layer of red chalk and then a very thick layer of brown carstone immediately above the beach. As you go south along the coast to Heacham and on to Snettisham, the topsoil and the chalk get thinner, until there is just a thin layer of soil. The carstone lies just under the surface of the fields. Ken Hill is where the land rises between Snettisham and the sea. The top of the hill is only 38 m above sea level, not very high as a hill but by far the highest point along the coast.

In the late 1940s after World War II, fields of poor soil around Ken Hill were used for growing lavender as they still are around Heacham today. Herbs like lavender, sage, thyme and rosemary need much less fertile soil than crops which are more 'hungry', like wheat, barley and potatoes. But when, after WWII, even poor land had to be brought into use for food crops, the fields on and around Ken Hill were brought into use by ploughing.

Lavender field on the edge of Ken Hill, Snettisham

In 1948, the farm-worker at Ken Hill farm was told to hitch a new deeper plough to his tractor and to plough the lavender field. He set off across the field. There was a 'clang' and he noticed a bit of metal in the turned-over soil. Thinking it was a bit of an old brass bedstead, he threw it into the grass at the side of the field and went on ploughing. Soon, he turned over another bit of metal which also went into the grass.

Before he left for home, he mentioned the bits of 'old brass bedstead' left in the hedge to his boss. When the manager of the Estate checked the bits of metal, he thought they looked a bit like gold. He consulted a friend who had a contact with the archaeology experts at the County Museum in Norwich.

Finding the first torc at Ken Hill – what the farm-worker told the local Paper

'On that day, I woke up, got dressed and fed the kids their breakfast. We've got a boy and a girl. When they had finished, I went to work at the farm – ploughing. The plough went deep and I found some bits of metal.

I did not know what it was, so at the end of the day, I told the Boss about it and went home. The next day was my day off but I got called in to the farm and they told me that I'd found the first ever torc in Snettisham. They told me it was made of gold but I just went home again as it really was my day off!

The next day, I got ready to go to work but a man from the Press came round to my house. I was so bothered that I called work and told them I couldn't come in. I stayed at home all day. By the next day, I realised that my life had changed as I was now famous because the torc I found would be known forever and would make Snettisham famous. But I did not want all the publicity and just kept quiet at home.

(by Chloe R.)

There is an old photograph, which we think may be a picture from the local paper, showing the man who did the ploughing. But we are not sure. He did not want the publicity and his identity is still not widely known. We shall respect his wish to remain anonymous, especially as we think as he may be a relative of one of our school staff!

This is the picture of the un-named ploughman.

That first find of gold on Ken Hill in 1948 was of a very damaged and battered torc which had been hit by the plough. Soon people were keen to see if they could find more gold. The owner of the field and the Norfolk Archaeological Survey wanted to prevent everyone getting access to the site which was on private land, so the exact location was not made public. Some people did find out and there was some illegal access to the field but the site was protected as much as possible so that further surveys could be carried out before treasure-hunters descended on the site and stole what they found.

There have been rumours that a large hoard of gold and silver coins was found on Ken Hill by an unauthorised metal detector and removed from the site without any record being kept. This was said to have been of over 6000 silver coins in a silver bowl and 500 gold coins and ingots which were buried beneath the bowl. If this rumour is true, all these coins have been lost. Sadly, we shall probably never know the truth of the matter.

3. Finding more torcs

More of the field was explored by experts who carefully scraped away the soil to reveal the carstone underneath. It soon became clear that more fragments of gold would not be found just lying around on the surface. Any that had been there for centuries would have been found long ago and taken away without any record being kept.

The archaeologists found that shallow pits had been dug into the surface of the carstone and it was in these pits that they found more gold. The first pieces of gold which had been ploughed up in 1948 were called 'Hoard A' and each successive find was given a letter B, C etc.

A pit in the stone containing a hoard of gold, as shown in the sign board in the centre of Snettisham village

The carstone is actually quite a soft sandstone and so it was not very difficult for the metal workers to hack out the rock to make these pits. Carstone is still quarried at Snettisham and there are many buildings in the villages which have been built of the brown stone, including our own school. In this photograph of the school wall, Lily W. and Leah Y. are pointing to the place where some naughty pupil has carved initials into the surface of the stone.

You can also see how soft the carstone is from the wall around St Mary's church graveyard, which is built from both flint and carstone.

The soft brown carstone has been eroded away by the weather whereas the hard grey flint is not eroded at all.

St Mary's Church is built mainly of limestone, much harder than the carstone. The enabled the medieval stone masons to build a parish church for Snettisham with a fine spire 175 foot tall which acts as a sea-mark for ships coming into the Wash to dock at King's Lynn.

The 175 foot spire of St Mary's Parish Church, Snettisham, from the graveyard.

Up on Ken Hill, the carstone just under the surface of the soil is just as soft as the stone used to build the school and many of the houses in the village. In 1950, a pit was found in the carstone with several gold torcs including the Great Torc, together with bracelets, rings and coins. These were used to date the items in the pit. This group of torcs and gold items was given the title Hoard B, as it was the second to be found. More gold items were brought up by ploughing and excavating in 1964, 1968 and 1973, by which time the Hoards had been labelled up to E.

In 1989, Squadron Leader Hodder was given permission by the land owner to search the site with his metal detector. At first, he just found metal fragments and single coins, rather than a hoard. But when he returned in the following year, he found something quite different in a hollow in the carstone. Someone had used a bronze container to hold a large collection of over 500 pieces of scrap metal, gold, silver and bronze.

The metal-worker had then buried the bronze container in the pit. It was as if the metal worker had collected all his off-cuts and fragments of precious metal for re-use and stored them away in a convenient container. He had then lodged it for safe-keeping in a cavity in the carstone, much as a modern jeweller would keep all his scrap gold and silver and store it in a safe place.

A team from the British Museum, helped by archaeologists from Norfolk Museums Service, decided that the next stage had to be the removal of all the top soil from the field in which torcs had been found. They used a metal box scraper dragged behind a tractor to strip off all the top-soil from an area of about three acres.

Five more pits in the carstone were revealed, each containing a hoard of metal objects (G-L). Some had clearly been disturbed by the tip of the plough but others had lain in the soil protected by the surrounding carstone for up to two thousand years.

Another Haiku by Callum E.

Finding more and more
To form the Snettisham hoards
Hidden for many years.

In the course of all these excavations between 1948 and today, an astonishing number of complete or damaged Celtic Iron Age gold, silver and bronze torcs have been found at Ken Hill. There have been nearly 180 of them, of which 75 have been found more or less complete. In addition, 100 other gold and silver items, 170 coins and very many pieces of scrap metal have been found. The Snettisham hoards taken together are the largest collection of Iron Age gold and precious metal ever found in Western Europe. In all there are about 30 kg in weight of gold and gold alloys. This is a hugely valuable collection of beautiful objects most of which are over two thousand years old.

Damaged tubular gold torc from the Snettisham hoards

Not all the torcs were of the 'twisted ropes of gold' pattern. Several were quite different and similar to torcs known to have been made in other parts of Europe, such as the two made out of thin gold sheet to form a tubular structure.

Included in one of the hoards were a number of gold coins known to have come from Gaul (what is now France) and dated to about 200 BC. These may well have been held as gold bullion ready to be melted down and worked by the Iceni into new torcs of the 'twisted rope' pattern. Other bronze coins found are known to have been made in Kent and are known as 'potin'. There must have been an extensive network of Celtic trading links across Britain and into Europe.

We know that the gold that was used by the Iceni craftsmen working on Ken Hill was not originally from Norfolk as there are no sources of gold in Norfolk.

4. Who made the Snettisham Torcs?

Archaeologists agree that the torcs found on Ken Hill were made by Iceni metal-workers between about 200 and 40 BC, but most from a period between 75 and 40 BC. They know this because they found coins with the torcs which could be dated from the designs on them. At that time the whole area was occupied by the Iceni, one of the many Celtic tribes we used to call 'Ancient Britons'.

The Iceni area of England by Millie G.

The Iceni occupied what is now the County of Norfolk, with part of Suffolk and the Peterborough area. Their home was effectively an island. The River Ouse running west and then north into the Wash and the River Waveney running east and then into the North Sea both rise in the same boggy area not far from Knettishall. The rivers still form the County boundary between Norfolk ('the North Folk') and Suffolk (the 'South Folk').

We do not know when the Iceni first lived in this area. Millions of years ago, what is now north-west Norfolk was covered by the sea. Beds of dead sea-creatures were built up layer by layer under the water. These beds eventually formed the chalk layers which now lie under the soil of Norfolk and can be dated from the fossil remains which they contain. The carstone is sandstone which was laid down from sandy sediments from the early Cretaceous period of about 110 million years ago. The red chalk and then white chalk have been built up in later periods about 100 million year ago, still millions of year before any humans lived in Norfolk.

From about 700,000 years ago to about 8,000 years ago, the whole area of Britain was covered with ice. We call this the Ice Age. But the climate was not always freezing cold. Sometimes, the ice melted and left the land covered with forests and moorland with giant animals living in what became Norfolk. We know about these animals from their bones which became fossilized in the deposits which still lie under the surface.

The fossil bones of a giant hippo almost twice the size of a modern hippo were found in the soil not far from Norwich. A wild storm at West Runton on the Norfolk coast washed a huge fossil bone from the soft cliff and left it lying on the beach where it was picked up by two walkers. When the bone was checked by the Museum Service, it was found to be part of a huge pre-historic elephant, a ten ton mammoth which once lived in the forests of North Norfolk.

Archaeologists now think that the first men and women who lived in Norfolk, the Neanderthals, could have lived among these giant animals. It is even possible that the West Runton elephant, whose fossilized bones were found on the beach, was killed by these first human hunters. It is much more likely that they killed smaller pre-historic prey, using weapons made from stone especially the stone which common in much of Norfolk, flint.

During the Ice Age, the moving glaciers left gravel in hollows in the land, gravel which has become valuable in recent times for building roads and making concrete. In one gravel pit, in Thetford Forest, parts of mammoth tusks and bones, and even a mammoth tooth, were found in 2002, together with a very fine flint hand-axe. This gravel pit is famous as the best Neanderthal site ever found in Britain with many hand-axes, fossil bones and even fossil insects found which have been dated to be about 65,000 years old.

After the climate warmed and the ice melted for the last time, men began to use trees to build huts and to travel in dug-out canoes, in what was an 'age of wood'. By about 4300 BC, people in the Norfolk area began to cultivate crops as well as hunt animals for food. This age of the first farmers has been called the New Stone Age, or Neolithic, because they made increasingly effective flint tools, stone axes, scrapers and arrowheads. They started to use clay to make pottery bowls by firing the clay and they buried their dead under long mounds of earth called barrows. There are very few barrows in West Norfolk but many more in the East of the County and around the Broads area.

Around 3200 BC, people living in Norfolk set up 'henges'. There were rings of large timber posts similar to the stone monument at Stone Henge in Wiltshire which is thought to date from about 3100 BC. The Norfolk timber 'henges' are much smaller. One has survived, at Arminghall, just south of Norwich.

In 1998, timbers were found on the beach near Holme and a bronze axe-head was found nearby. There was a lot of excitement about the discovery of this so-called 'Sea Henge'. But it was different from the timber 'henges' found in other parts of the County. It was an oval ring of timber posts with a central oak trunk set upside down in the mud and dated to about 2050 BC. It must have stood on an island off the coast as the sea has risen since then. The purpose of this monument remains a mystery – perhaps it was a way for men to connect with the underworld.

'Sea-henge' discovered on the beach near Holme next the Sea

The bronze axes associated with these monuments probably would not have been made in Norfolk, but were brought in from the south-west of England. That is where the ores of copper and tin were found in abundance. These are the two metals from which bronze was made. In Norfolk, men went on using flint tools throughout the Bronze Age, roughly 3200 to 600 BC, because flint was so readily available.

About 30 miles to the south-east of Snettisham, in the sandy Breckland soil, there is an area called Grimes Graves, open heathland pock-marked with depressions like shell-holes. These hollows are not actually graves at all. They are the remains of ancient flint mines, where the soil and chalk have been dug away to form mine shafts up to 15m deep. These enabled the miners to reach the layers of flint in the chalk. They brought the nodules of flint back up to the surface where they could be worked on. The mine shafts have, over the centuries, filled in with soil and chalk, leaving depressions across the land.

Grimes Graves, the hollows left by Bronze Age flint mining

The shallow mines have been dated from about 2675 BC to 2200 BC, in the middle of the Bronze Age in England. The lumps of flint which were dug out and brought to the surface were then broken open. The pieces of flint could then be 'knapped', hit with other stones to flake off slithers of flint to form axes, arrow-heads and spear-heads. All these items were not just useful to the Norfolk people. They could be traded with the people of other areas who did not have a ready supply of flint.

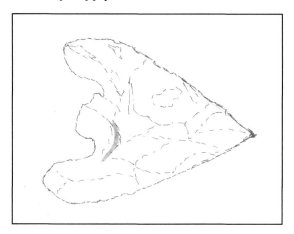

Bronze Age flint arrowhead drawn by Harry C.

One of the mysteries of prehistoric Norfolk is what happened in the centuries after about 1800 BC in the late Bronze Age up to the start of the Iron Age around 700 BC. If people were living in the area at this time, they left very little evidence in the form of pottery or dwelling sites. Dateable bronze objects have been found, but where did the people live? The oldest gold jewellery found in Norfolk, in the form of gold rings and bracelets, has also been dated from this period.

Living in the Bronze Age

We know that, in the Bronze Age, people lived in round houses with a central fire for heating and cooking. They would eat food like Emmer wheat, barley, lentils and bitter vetch. They had to learn how to spin yarn from wool on a spindle. The clothes people made out of this wool showed where they came from and whether they were rich or poor. The wheel had been invented and people could use horses to draw carts. Only rich people could afford bronze tools. For a long time, poorer farmers and craftsmen continued to use flint tools to do their work.

(by Megan D.)

After the Stone Age and the Bronze Age, the next big breakthrough of technology in Britain was the coming of the Iron Age. Archaeologists think that iron was first smelted from rocks somewhere in what we now call the Middle East around 1400 BC. The new metal was harder, stronger and lighter than bronze and iron weapons could be given sharper edges giving users of iron an advantage in fighting. From the Middle East, iron-smelting spread west. People in Britain were using iron from about 800 BC.

With the spread of iron-working came a spread of people, out from Europe north of the Alps and across the Channel and on into Ireland. These Iron Age people are now known as the Celts and one theory was that they spread from Central Europe north into the British Isles, south and west into the Spanish peninsular and east into Greece and Turkey, taking their Celtic languages with them.

An alternative view is that the Celts started in a language zone to the west of the British Isles, NW France and Spain and spread east across Europe. No-one seems to know which theory is correct, but we now call the many similar groups of people who lived in the west of Spain, France, Britain and Ireland, the Celts.

Whichever theory proves correct, both are based on the similarities between the languages and the art of peoples who are now classified together as Celts. These include the many distinct tribes who were living in England before the Roman conquest who used to be called the 'Ancient Britons'. In the area we call Norfolk, the tribe was the Iceni. To the south, lived the Trinovantes and the Corieltavi and Catuvellauni lived to the north and west.

If the Snettisham torcs were made between 75 and 40 BC, they must have been made by Iceni metal-workers, just before the Romans invaded England, towards the end of the Iron Age.

5. What do we know about the Iceni ?

The Iceni left very little evidence of their occupation of the Snettisham area in the late Iron Age, except for their coins, their jewelry, and what other people, especially their enemies, wrote about them.

They lived in little round houses with straw roofs, held down with wooden pegs. Their house walls were made of mud, all stuck together with horse manure and animal hair. The floor would have been made of mud too. Inside the house, there was a fire pit with wooden benches either side to sit on.

(by Ruby H. and Chloe R.)

Over the following centuries, all these materials rot down quite quickly, unlike the bricks and stones from which later houses and castles were built, so the Iceni left little trace for archaeologists to find.

Replica Iron Age hut of the type the Iceni would have lived in

As far as we know, the Iceni did not use writing so there are no inscriptions on stone or wood which could have survived over two thousand years.

They left no tombstones and seemed not to have buried their dead as no burial mounds, barrows or even single graves have been found. Archaeologists believe that they exposed their dead on platforms open to the sky so that bodies would decompose and the remains be eaten by foxes, wolves or birds, much as the North American Indian peoples exposed their dead.

They did leave earth bank fortifications, some with double ditches, probably topped with a timber palisade. There are several in NW Norfolk, such as the 'castle' in Thetford and the circular remains at Warham Camp near the Norfok coast. Some of these Iceni earthworks are in a line, such as the earthworks in West Norfolk, the Bichamditch, Fossditch and the Black Ditches, roughly in a NS line west of Thetford.

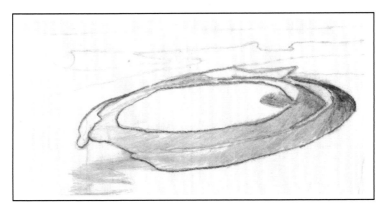

Sketch of the earth ramparts of Warham Camp by Jasmin D.

Warham is an Iron Age fort thought to have been built by the Iceni with a double ditch and mounds enclosing a roughly circular area. It is on the north Norfolk coast next to the River Stiffney.

We also know that the Iceni had horses and that horses were a very important part of their culture. Many of the Iron Age metal items which have been found in Norfolk have some connection with the use of horses, such as harness and cart fittings, bits for horses mouths, rings through which the reins ran and linchpins which held the cart wheels on the end of the axle. Some of the rings are made of bronze and have Celtic style enamel decoration. An Iron Age bridle bit was found which had beautiful enamelled decoration, with different designs on each side of the bit.

All these items are typical of the Iceni area. It seems that the Iceni had a very special relationship with the horses they rode and those they used to pull their chariots. They really were the Iron Age 'people of the horse'.

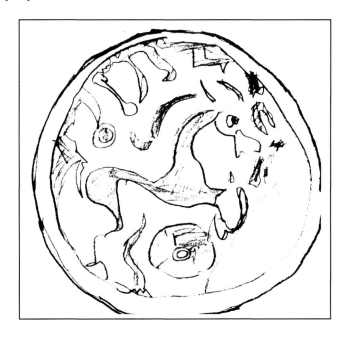

Drawing of an Iceni gold coin, a 'stater', showing a horse and a chariot wheel, by Mithu B.: actual size: about 14mm.

No-where else is this more clear than on Iceni gold coins of the late Iron Age. Many have been found which are of the 'face-horse' type, with a human face on one side and a picture of a horse on the other. This is often a picture of a very lively horse, sometimes with the wheel of a chariot beside it, like the one which Mithu has drawn.

Not all the Iceni gold coins found so far have come from Norfolk. The largest hoard of Iceni gold coins ever found, believed to date from about 40 BC to about AD 15 was found in Suffolk. These gold 'staters' are just part of the hoard. They show the typical Iceni decorations of horses, wheels and New Moons.

Other Iceni coins have been found with pictures of a wild boar on one side, or with a picture of a wolf. Some are silver coins; many are gold. Some have been found by metal detectors as single coins. Others have been found as large hoards, including a hoard of 340 silver coins found buried in a clay pot in a field at Honningham.

The earliest of these Iceni face/horse coins have no inscriptions, just a side view, a profile of a human face, almost a caricature. When the Romans invaded Britain, they brought with them Roman coins which had the image of the Roman Emperor and lettering to show which Emperor was depicted.

Two sides of a Roman coin of the Emperor Claudius
who invaded Britain in AD 43

Later Iceni coins, particularly from the time of the Iceni King Prasutagus showed a picture of the King, with a crude inscription on one side and a realistic image of a horse on the other, rather than a stylised earlier Iceni horse. These coins may well have been made by a metal-worker heavily influenced by the Romans, especially as they also have the crude inscription ESIGO FECIT – 'made by Esigo' on the horse side.

Celtic prancing horses from a copper bucket found in Kent, drawn
by Mithu B.

Celtic people loved to use stylised images of animals and birds, flowing, swirling patterns and interlocking shapes in their designs. Typical of this style is the use of what seem to be prancing horses with strange lips and almost human feet which was found on the upper band of a copper bucket from Kent, dated 75-25 BC.

Other Celtic designs use interwoven circles to form an overall triangle:

Celtic design of interconnecting rings drawn by Harry C.

In Northern Britain, in what is now Northumberland, Celtic art survived much later than in Norfolk where the coming of the Anglo-Saxons swept away the influence of the Celtic tribes. At Lindisfarne, off the Northumberland coast on land that becomes an island at high tide, the monks of the Priory used the same swirling rings and stylised creatures to decorate their Gospels.

This wonderful manuscript which still survives today was created around 700 AD, much later than the Iceni period of Norfolk, but still shows Celtic influences. The monks used bright colours and included sea-birds, dogs and even human faces.

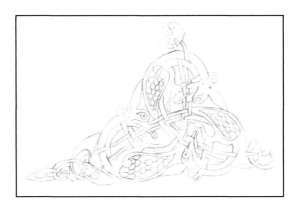

Celtic design with birds and swirling patterns from the Lindisfarne Gospels, drawn by Megan D.

So we know that the Iceni were a very artistic people, capable of very high quality metal-work in gold and silver, decorated with brightly coloured enamel work. They kept horses and used them in light wicker-work chariots for fighting. Their iron swords were long and heavy, with two handed grips and sharp edges, good for slashing and cutting as the Iceni warrior charged into battle either on foot or in a light chariot.

We also know that they were a very religious people. Their priests were the Druids, the teachers, healers and arbitrators of the tribe, respected for their wisdom. Their rituals included sacrifice, both animal and human, and their sacred places were often groves of oak trees or associated with mistletoe. They would advise the Iceni kings on legal disputes and pass on their knowledge of tribal customs from generation to generation. They also composed poetry, a tradition which is still preserved in the Welsh Eisteddfod, the national celebration of music and poetry held every year.

These Druids were always men, not women. They preserved an air of power and mystery around their activities, offering mysticism and magic and acting as the human link between the people and the world of the spirits.

What a Celtic Druid might have looked like

They could banish individuals from the tribal area and negotiate with enemies on behalf of the people. They were in many ways the glue that held the people together within a Celtic community.

Gold and Iron on Ken Hill

One of the most interesting findings of the excavations of the field on Ken Hill where the gold torcs were found was a ditch across the site. This ditch seemed to separate an area on one side of the ditch where the pits in the carstone had been made to keep the hoards of gold and silver, and a wider area where there was evidence of iron smelting.

The smelting of iron ore with charcoal and a blast of air was a skill well known to the Iceni. They had an abundant supply of charcoal from the woodland on Ken Hill. The carstone was itself a source of iron as an iron-rich sandstone – the brown colour is itself evidence of iron in the rock. They also had access to other sources of iron ores within their own territory, especially up on the high ground behind the North Norfolk coast around Sheringham.

The ditch across the Ken Hill field was also interesting because it contained a quantity of iron-smelting slag, the waste product of iron making. This suggests that the Iceni had established on one side of the ditch their workshops for producing the beautiful torcs for which Snettisham is famous. On the other side they set up their iron-smelting furnaces, small smelting sites known as 'bloomeries' which produced the iron they needed for weapons, tools and the iron parts of their horse harnesses and chariots.

If this is true, Ken Hill in Iceni times must have been a hive of industry, on one side a 'Birmingham' or 'Sheffield' of the Iceni where iron was smelted and weapons forged. On the other side of the ditch, a 'precious metals' quarter much as the city of Birmingham has had its jewelry quarter right up to today and London has a zone for goldsmiths and jewellers around Hatton Gardens.

Ken Hill must have been a place of fire and smoke, a wide clearing in the trees on the top of the hill, with men tapping away in small thatched workshops turning out beautiful gold torcs with extraordinary skill using the most basic of tools. It would have been a place of secrecy and mystery from which women and children may have been excluded. Druids may have presided over the whole operation ensuring that the spirits of the woods and of the fire looked kindly on the work. Perhaps they even sacrificed animals to ensure that the winning of iron from the rock and the turning of gold coins into torcs came out well.

And why did they hack out the pits or 'nests' in the carstone and bury their gold and silver in these pits? Some have suggested that these were 'votive offerings', sacrifices to the Gods of items of great worth, and that may have been true. But surely the existence of these 'pits' also has a much more everyday explanation. The

Iceni would have needed safe storage places, the equivalent of modern 'bank vaults'. In a world with no stone buildings and where raids from other tribes could take away portable wealth, the Ken Hill site would have needed secure places for valuables.

Just as a modern town has branches of banks, Barclays, Lloyds and HSBC, along the High Street, each with its safe deposit boxes, the Iceni had their carstone 'nests' on Ken Hill to serve the same purpose. Iceni metal workers could have used 'pits' in the carstone just as the vaults under Hatton Gardens serve the jewellers of London. Safe that is until a team of robbers with a concrete cutter breaks through from a neighboring cellar and steals the valuables, as happened recently in London.

A place of fire and smoke and also a very secret place, where men skilled in the mystery of getting iron out of stone would work well away from the village down below. Ken Hill is still a secret place, a private place, from which the public are excluded as the sign on the access road makes very clear.

There is no indication even that this is the road to the Ken Hill estate. Once gold has been found, even if it was many years ago, others may be tempted to try to look again and those who live and work on Ken Hill do not want that today. They ask others to respect their privacy.

But to the south, where Snettisham Common runs around the base of Ken Hill, there is public access. A very attractive footpath popular with dog walkers and joggers contours around the base of the hill, overlooking the farmland running down to the shore of the Wash.

The path around the foot of Ken Hill.

Ancient oak trees at the foot of Ken Hill

The path runs along the edge of the ancient woodlands that still cover the hill, where old oak and beech trees climb up to the crest. On a clear day, you can see right across the Wash from this footpath to the Lincolnshire coastline. The tower of Boston Stump, the tower of the parish church of St Botolph's, provides a sea-mark on that coast much as the spire of St Mary's, Snettisham does on the Norfolk shore.

Hidden away in the trees, where the shoulder of Lodge Hill looks down to the shore, stand the ruins of an old stone watch tower. Thought to date from the 1400s, the tower would have enabled a watch to have been kept on the shoreline to give warning of any invasion, much as the Iceni, centuries before, would have kept watch for Anglo-Saxon long-ships coming into the Wash and the Great Ouse River. In their turn, the Anglo-Saxon settlers would have watched for the Danish invaders to come to the coast of Norfolk in the 9th Century and in the 20th coastal watchers kept watch for Nazi Germany to attempt a landing on the shore of England.

6. The coming of the Romans

The Celtic tribes of Britain, including the Iceni, lived with little more than inter-tribal border disputes until their whole world change dramatically with the coming of the Romans. First to cross the Channel was Julius Caesar with an army of Roman Legions. He had already conquered and occupied Gaul, roughly what is now France, and he was aware that much of the support for those he had to fight in Gaul, actually came from the Celts across the Channel. He was determined to stop this. He also knew that Britain would provide him with good supplies of corn, always vital for feeding Roman armies, and supplies of other useful materials, including metals.

In 55 BC and again in 54 BC, Julius Caesar took his Legions across the Channel and invaded the south coast of Britain. He wrote a detailed Latin account of this campaign in his book, *Gallic Wars*, which is still available in English translation today. In Book 4 of this, he wrote a vivid description of the use which the Celtic tribes in Britain made of chariots for fighting against his Roman Legions:

'Their mode of fighting with their chariots is this: firstly they drive about in all directions and throw their weapons and generally break the ranks of the enemy with the very dread of their horses and the noise of their wheels; when they have worked themselves in between the troops of horse, they leap from their chariots and engage on foot.

The charioteers in the mean time withdraw some little distance from the battle, and so place themselves with their chariots that, if

*their masters are overpowered by the... enemy, they may have a
ready retreat to their own troops. Thus they display in battle the
speed of the horse and the firmness of infantry; by daily practice
...they are accustomed to check their horses at full speed and turn
them in an instant,run along the pole, stand on the yoke and thence
betake themselves at high speed their chariots again...'*
(Julius Caesar: Gallic Wars Book 4 Chapter 33, translated)

Caesar obviously had a respect for the Britons as fighters and
their ability to dash into action and then withdraw to safety when
pressed. Although Caesar defeated a Celtic tribal army in a major
battle in Kent, he did not conquer the rest of the Island. When
news of trouble in Gaul reached him, he decided to take his
Legions back over the Channel to sort out the Gauls.

Almost a century later, in 43 AD, the Roman Emperor Claudius
needed a victory to boost his power in Rome. He and his General,
Aulus Plautius, organised a full scale invasion of Britain with
50,000 Roman troops, four full Legions and all their supporting
cavalry and auxilaries. They landed on the South Coast and
marched north. The Britons responded by assembling an army of
resistance, led by the Catuvellauni, under the leadership of
Caractacus and his brother Togodumnus.

The two armies met near the River Medway. The Roman
victory changed the Celtic world of Southern Britain for four
hundred years. Togodumnus was killed. Caractacus withdrew to
the Thames but was then defeated a second time and fled to
continue the resistance to the Romans from the remote safety of
the Welsh hills.

The Iceni and the other defeated Celtic tribes to the north of the
Thames met with Plautius at the town of Camulodunum and
accepted defeat, becoming client kingdoms of Rome. They were
allowed to run their own affairs in their own territories, including
using their own coinage, and to follow their own tribal laws and

traditions, but their leaders had to recognise that they could only rule under the Romans' overall control.

As the Iceni did not themselves have written histories, most of what we know about them is from the writings of their enemies, the Romans. Julius Caesar described how they fought in chariots. Two other writers take up the story of events in Britain in the early years of Roman rule, the Roman historian Tacitus and a Greek writer who wrote a history of Rome in Latin, Cassius Dio. Tacitus wrote his Annals around 110 AD, at least fifty years after the events he describes. He at least had the advantage of being the father-in-law to the Roman General who was involved in those events, a soldier who later served as Governor of Britain.

Dio wrote much later, some time around 200-220 AD, nearly two centuries after Claudius invaded. He probably had a copy of Tacitus' work with him when he wrote. Neither of these two writers had much sympathy for the Britons. They wrote history from the point of view of the side who won, the Roman victors in the struggle between the Romans and the Celtic peoples.

The first sign of trouble was four years after the Claudian invasion. The Roman military commander wanted to ensure that the tribes who had become 'clients' of Rome did not have the ability to rebel while he was busy elsewhere. He did not have enough troops to ensure peace everywhere so he decided to disarm them. They could keep their hunting spears, knives and arrows but their swords were taken away from them.

The Iceni were incensed at this loss – their swords were part of their status as men and warriors. Heavy and two edged, with a two handed handle, they were weapons for slashing and hacking at enemies, terrifying in the hands of an warrior rushing towards you, waving his sword around his head.

Drawing of an Iceni longsword by Jack I.

The Roman military commander responded quickly and crushed the revolt. The Iceni lost the right to carry their swords, but the rebellion brought them together and they united under their King, Prasutagus. He brought some stability to the tribe and even had coins issued with his image on one side. His wife was a woman whose name is known to this day, Boudica, or as some people knew her, Boadicea.

Boudica's life

Boudica was born around 30 AD, we think in south-east England. Her parents were Diras (father) and Locrinus (mother). She grew up in the Iceni tribe. When the Roman Emperor Claudius sent a large Roman Army to invade Southern Britain in AD 43, she would have been a young girl of about 13.

(by Aimee K. and Oscar W.)

What Boudica might have looked like when she was about 13 years old by Anna Belle H.

More trouble for the Iceni

The Iceni, like several other tribes, had made a treaty with the Roman Procurator (Governor) but Roman traders began to come into their area. The Iceni resented this and wanted nothing to do with them.

Some time after the Roman Invasion, Prasutagus married Boudica. They had two daughters. When King Prasutagus died in AD 60 or 61, he left Boudica to reign as Queen. In his will, he also left his wealth to be shared equally between the Roman Emperor and his two daughters. But the Roman Procurator said that Prasutagus' will was not valid because the Emperor could not share with barbarians. The Romans ignored the will and took all the wealth and Iceni land by force for themselves.

Boudica protested about the soldiers taking everything. Procurator Decianus had her arrested, whipped and her daughters abused in front of her. The Roman continue to take lands and goods, sending the wealthy as well as the peasants into slavery. Boudica wanted revenge.

(by Aimee K. and Oscar W.)

Cassius Dio included a description of Boudica in his Annals:

'In stature she was very tall, in appearance most terrifying, in the glance of her eye most fierce, and her voice was harsh; a great mass of the tawniest hair fell to her hips; around her neck was a large golden necklace; and she wore a tunic of many colours over which a thick mantle was fastened with a brooch.'

(Cassius Dio *Annals LXII.2* in translation)

This was Boudica, the Iceni Queen, complete with gold torc at her neck. But what is the correct version of her name?

Boudica or Boadicea?

In the manuscripts of Tacitus, her name is recorded as Boudicca. He added a second c to the correct spelling in the language of the Iceni, which was 'Boudica'. The Iceni spoke the language of the Celtic tribes called 'Common Britannic'. Then someone copying out Tacitus's account by hand in medieval times misread the u for an a and the second c as an e, so as the result of these copying errors, by the time of the Victorians, Boudicca had become Boadicea.

(By Kacey B. and Adam R.)

The name actually mean 'victory' in the language of the Iceni. Because the British Queen Victoria had the same name, the story of Boadicea was revived in Victorian England and a statue to her was commissioned. It still stands by Westminster Bridge in London, just by the Houses of Parliament, Boadicea riding in her chariot, with her two daughters. But this statue is an inaccurate as the name of the Iceni Queen.

Statue of Boadicea opposite the Houses of Parliament in London

She is riding in a heavy war-chariot with knives spinning on the axle ends. Her horses are large war-horses, because the artists used a pair of Victorian riding-horses as models for his work. But the Queen of the Iceni would have ridden in a light whicker-work chariot drawn by light and nimble ponies, like the one shown in our drawing below and like the replica chariot in the Museum in Norwich Castle. This chariot is part of an excellent display showing Boudica as she really was, not Boadicea as the Victorians wanted her to be.

Boudica on her war chariot by Anna Belle H.

Tacitus continues the story of the Iceni's response:

'Exasperated by their acts of violence, and dreading worse calamities, the Icenians took up arms. The Trinobantians joined in the revolt. The neighboring states, not as yet taught to crouch in bondage, pledged themselves, in secret councils, to stand forth in the cause of liberty. What chiefly fired their indignation was the conduct of the Roman veteran soldiers, lately planted as a colony at Camulodunum. These men treated the Britons with cruelty and oppression; they drove the natives from their houses, and calling them by the [shameful] names of slaves and captives, added insult to their tyranny. In these acts of oppression, the veterans were supported by the common soldiers; a set of men, by their habits of life, trained to licentiousness, and, in their turn, expecting to reap the same advantages.

(from Tacitus Annals Chapter 31 in translation)

Boudica's revenge was swift. The Iceni rebels and the Celtic tribes around them, a great horde of Celtic fighters, descended on the Roman garrison town of Camulodunum (modern Colchester). It was full of Roman women and children and only lightly defended by Roman veterans. Tacitus tells us that:

'Unguarded and unprepared, they were taken by surprise, and, overpowered by the Barbarians in one general assault. The colony was laid waste with fire and sword. The temple held out, but, after a siege of two days, was taken by storm.....

Autumn D. of Birch Class has imagined that she has been an archaeologist working on the remains of Roman Colchester:

'I've just got back from exploring Colchester and all I could find was black and grey dusty ashes everywhere. There were a few remains of buildings and metal. I coughed a lot and sneezed a few times – you could tell it had all been destroyed; buildings were black because they'd been burnt down.

There were some bones and skeletons. I found a skull with an old rotten iron sword still stuck in it. You could tell it must have been easy for the Iceni to destroy the city because it looked so broken, as if no-one had tried to stop the Celts.'

Madelyne and Cerys describe what happened when the Commander of the Roman Ninth Hispana Legion heard the news of the burning of Colchester or Camulodunum as the Romans called it.

'The Ninth Hispana Legion were stationed on the eastern edge of Iceni territory. They were guarding the crossing of the River Nene at Longthorpe, near modern Peterborough. When news of the revolt reached him, their commander thought he would only need half of his soldiers because the Iceni were not very strong and

were led by a woman. So they left half the Legion behind in their camp when they marched off through the forests to face the Iceni.

One by one, the Iceni killed the Romans that were sent, one by one. There was no big battle, just a spear in the back or sudden cutting of a throat as their line of march went through the trees. Of the men of the Ninth Hispana who set out from Longthorpe, none survived; only the ones who stayed in the camp were left. The rest were slaughtered by the Iceni. This was the first time that a Roman Legion was defeated in Britain.'

Legio IX Hispana at a re-enactment at Longthorpe Tower

In Peterborough today, a group of enthusiasts have set up a re-enactment of the Legion, the Legio IX Hispana. They were called 'Hispana' because they were recruited from Spain. The men in their 'Legion' have equipped themselves with splendid body armour, swords and javelins, just as the Legion would have over two thousand years ago. They take part in displays of Roman military tactics in re-enactments of battles across the region.

The site of the IXth Legion's fort at Longthorpe has been discovered on a golf course just next to the Ferry Meadows park. Archeaologists have found that it was rebuilt after the news of the defeat was sent back to their camp, but the new fort was only half the original size.

The Ninth Hispana Legion was eventually brought back to its full strength after this disaster and sent north to York (Roman Eboracum). When there was another rebellion north of Hadrian's Wall, the Ninth Hispana set out again to quell the rebels. This time, not just half the Legion was killed, none of them came back. Worst of all, they lost their Eagle, the bronze symbol of their Roman pride. It was never found and the Ninth Hispana was never reformed.

From Camulodunum the Iceni and their allies surged on to attack the city of Londinium, modern London. Again poorly defended and full of merchants and their families, Londinium was very vulnerable. The Iceni captured the city easily and again sacked it, burning the buildings to the ground and massacring the population.

News of these disasters was sent south to Rome and north to the Island of Anglesey. Cassius Dio takes up the story:

'.....a terrible disaster occurred in Britain. Two cities were sacked, eighty thousand of the Romans and of their allies perished, and the island was lost to Rome. Moreover, all this ruin was brought upon the Romans by a woman, a fact which in itself caused them the greatest shame. Boudica, a Briton woman of the royal family and possessed of greater intelligence than often *belongs to women. This woman assembled her army, to the number of some 120,000.'*

(Cassius Dio *Annals LXII* in translation)

Camulodunum and Londinium, two major centres of Roman power, had fallen. Boudica's army then turned north up the road the Romans had built called Watling Street, roughly on the line of our M1. They reached the third Roman stronghold, the city of Verulamium, now St Albans, the second largest town in Roman Britain. Her army again over-ran the city, sacking and burning it, just as they had done to the other Roman settlements and again the archaeologists have found the evidence in a layer of ash.

Tacitus provides an explanation of why these cities were left so exposed to the anger of the Iceni. The Roman Governor of Britain was busy, away on a campaign of his own:

'.....a dreadful calamity befell the army in Britain. Paulinus Suetonius succeeded to the command; a distinguished officer...whose military talents made him confident who was raised to the highest eminence ....by the voice of the people. By subduing the mutinous spirit of the Britons he hoped to equal the brilliant success of (other generals.) With this ambition, he decided to subdue the isle of Mona; a place inhabited by a warlike people, and a common refuge for all the discontented Britons.'

'Mona' was the Isle of Anglesey, off the north-west coast of Wales, and Suetonius had marched his Legions up Watling Street to subdue the island. It was the last stronghold of the Druids, the fanatical religious leaders of the Celtic tribes. Suetonius had to cross the Menai Straits to get to the island:

'On the opposite shore stood the Britons, in a mass of men prepared for action. Women were seen running through the ranks in wild disorder; their clothes were black; their hair loose to the wind, in their hands flaming torches, and their whole appearance

resembling the frantic rage of the Furies. The Druids were lined up behind them, with hands uplifted, praying to their gods, and shouting horrible appeals for their help. The novelty of the fight struck the Romans with awe and terror. They stood in stupid amazement, as if their limbs were frozen riveted to one spot, a target for the enemy.

But their General's encouragement spread new vigour through the ranks, and the men, by mutual reproaches, spurred each other on to deeds of courage. They realised that they would be disgraced if they yielded to a troop of women, and a band of fanatic priests; so they advanced their standards, and rushed on to the attack with impetuous fury.

The Britons perished in the flames, which they themselves had kindled. The island fell, and a garrison was established to hold it in Roman control. The religious groves, dedicated to superstition and barbarous rites, were levelled to the ground. In those woods, the natives [had stained] their altars with the blood of their prisoners, and looked for clues about the will of their gods in the guts of men..

While Suetonius was employed in making his arrangements to secure the island, he received intelligence that Britain had revolted, and that the whole province was up in arms.
(Cassius Dio Annals LXII.2 in translation)

Suetonius did march south as fast as he could with some of his army and nearly got to Londinium and Verulamium in time to meet Boudica's forces. But he had heard of the fate of the Ninth Hispana Legion and he decided he had too few of his soldiers to engage Boudica in battle. He left the two cities to their fate, turning back north again to meet up with as many of his Legions as he could muster. He planned to concentrate his forces for a final battle at a place of his own choosing, a site which gave as much advantage as possible to the disciplined and heavily armoured Roman legionaries.

The two armies met somewhere along the line of Watling Street. Exactly where is still debated but most think that it was near to the village of Mancetter on the edge of Atherstone in what is now Warwickshire. The Celtic army was huge, nearly a quarter of a million led by a woman, fighting for honour and freedom but lacking discipline and organisation. Many carried eight foot spears with heavy iron spearheads, and flat double edged swords, their sacred swords, three feet long.

In front of the army, the Celtic carnyx players, the war-trumpeters, blew a challenge to the Roman. These were the Celtic equivalent of the Pipers who have led Highland Regiments and the bugle-players of the Royal Marines, musicians to lead troops into battle.

Carnyx playing Celtic warriors wearing leather trousers, from the decorations on the rim of the Gundestrup cauldron, a silver bowl dating from 150-50 BC found in a Danish bog. It shows scenes from Iron Age Celtic life.

The head of a carnyx, a Celtic war trumpet with
a clattering tongue, drawn by Dylan J.

These war-trumpets, the Celtic Carnyx, were tall metal shafts
with mouthpieces like trumpets and fearsome heads, part dragon,
part wolf, with red clattering tongues. The noise they made was
designed to strike terror into their enemies and to give courage to
the Celts.

Meanwhile, the Romans were already in position, drawn up in
a solid line between two areas of woods so that the Iceni would be
funnelled down towards them. Suetonius had one full Legion, the
XIVth, with some soldiers from the XXth Legion and auxiliaries
drawn from garrisons along Watling Street. It was a Roman army
of about 10,000 battle hardened, disciplined troops in their full kit
of helmet, body armour, belt and apron of leather. They carried
curved shields with bronze edges and an iron boss. Each man had
two javelins, throwing spears over six feet long, and a short
stabbing sword.

They had trained for years in fighting drills, forming tightly
locked shields for defence and wedge shaped attack formations.
They were outnumbered almost 25 to 1 and they needed every help
the landscape could offer. Paulinus had chosen a defensive position

with thick forest on each side and a narrow plain in front. The Romans could stand and block any advance and the Iceni could not make full use of their overwhelming numbers on such a narrow front.

Tacitus puts into Boudica's mouth a rousing speech to her troops as she wore her gold torc and rode her chariot in front of the Iceni army:

Boudica, in a [chariot], with her two daughters before her, drove through the ranks. She harangued the different nations in their turn:

'This,' she said, 'is not the first time that the Britons have been led to battle by a woman. But now I do not come to boast the pride of a long line of ancestry, nor even to recover my kingdom and the plundered wealth of my family.

I take the field, like the meanest among us, to uphold the cause of freedom, and to seek revenge for my body marked with the stripes of whipping and my two daughters shamefully raped. From the pride and arrogance of the Romans nothing is sacred; all are subject to violation.

But the Gods' revenge is now on our side. A Roman legion dared to face the warlike Britons: with their lives they paid for their rashness; none survived the carnage of that day, except a messenger who fled to hide in their camp, desperate to save himself by running away. As we prepare to fight and shout our war-cries, the Romans, even now, shrink back with terror.

What will happen when the battle starts? Look around, and see how many we are. We are proud to display our warlike spirits, and know that we draw our swords for vengeance. On this spot we must either conquer, or die with glory. There is no alternative.

Though a woman, my resolution is fixed: the men, if they please, may choose to survive and live in slavery.'

(Tacitus Annals Book 35 in translation)

According to Tacitus, in a moment of such importance, Suetonius did not remain silent. He ridiculed the enemy and urged his men to valour, inspiring and encouraging them to stand firm and face the inevitable attack.

'Despise,' he said, 'the savage uproar, the yells and shouts of undisciplined Barbarians. In that mixed multitude, the women out-number the men. They lack discipline and are poorly armed. They are not soldiers who come to offer battle; they are bastards, runaways, the refuse of your swords, who have often fled before you, and will again take to their heals when they see your ranks which have conquered so many times before. .

In all engagements it is the valour of a few that turns the fortune of the day. It will be your immortal glory, that with a scanty number you can equal the exploits of a great and powerful army. Keep your ranks; discharge your javelins; rush forward to a close attack; bear down all with your bucklers, and hack a way through with your swords. Pursue the vanquished, and never think of spoil and plunder. Conquer, and victory gives you everything.'

(Tacitus Annals Book 36 in translation)

Kian S. takes up the story of the start of the great battle:

'There were about 250,000 Celts led by the woman, Boudica, to fight the Romans. The Celts had no armour apart from leather trousers and they covered themselves in blue paint called woad. The Romans had metal armour, helmets with cheek pieces on the side and heavy plates on their shoulders and chests to protect them. They had rectangular shields which were curved to cover the

whole body and they could lock them together to make a wall of shields.'

This is how Ruby H. and Ruby W. described the battle, with help from Kian:

'The Romans were outnumbered by the Celts by about twenty five to one. But they were highly trained and could lock shields. They formed a long solid line between two woods and stood silently, silent like the mist hanging in the air.

The hyperactive Celts charged at them, but the Romans stood. When the Celts got close, the Romans threw their spears, ten thousand spears into a great mass of Celtic fighters, killing thousands at a time.

The Roman stood. When the Celts charged again, each Roman threw his second spear, ten thousand spears into a great mass of Celtic fighters.

Then the Romans started to push forward. They formed a wedge with their shields and forced the Celts back. Using their short stabbing swords, the Romans could kill Celts pressed against their line and, slowly, the Celts started to falter.

Before the battle, they had brought their women and children with them and left them in a line of carts to keep them safe across the rear of their army. But this now worked against them as the Romans pushed them back. They were trapped against the line of carts. The Celts could not run away and in the end about eighty thousand Celts died. Out of the ten thousand Romans who fought the battle only four hundred were killed and about the same number wounded.

The Romans had finally defeated Boudica and her rebellious Celts.'

Tacitus tells us that '*men and women, even their cattle and horses, fell in the carnage and were added to the heaps of slain. ....The glory of the day was equal to the most splendid victory of ancient times'.* (*Tacitus Annals Book 36 in translation*)

Boudica was said by some to have ended her own life by taking poison. The Iceni never again rebelled against Rome. The ringleaders were rounded up and executed. Boudica's revolt had taken thousands of men away from their homes and their farms in the early spring and summer and no crops had been planted. Starvation added to the ignominy of defeat.

The Romans built a new town just outside where Norwich is now and called it *'Venta Icenorum',* the capital or meeting place of the Iceni, but it was not an Iceni settlement. Archaeologists have found the site of the town in the Tas valley near Caistor St Edmund, just south of Norwich. It was a Roman town, and is still marked as such on today's maps, a symbol of Roman domination of the area. The Iceni had been pacified and the revolt which Boudica had led ended in total defeat.

There were no more gold torcs made on Ken Hill just outside Snettisham after about 61 AD, the year of the revolt. A hoard of bronze bowls has been found at Crownthorpe which have been dated from the time of the Iceni revolt. It seems that they were buried in the ground to avoid their capture by the rebels as they are of Roman design. Other hoards from this time contain silver drinking cups and silver coins, again presumably buried in a time of instability. Roman occupation brought the Iceni's long tradition of metal working to an end.

7. Where did the Iceni gold come from?

Included in one of the hoards found on Ken Hill, were a number of gold coins known to have come from Gaul (what is now France) and dated about 200 BC. These may well have been held as gold bullion ready to be melted down and worked by the Iceni into new torcs of the 'twisted rope' pattern. What we do know is that the gold that was used by the Iceni craftsmen working on Ken Hill was not originally from Norfolk as there are no sources of gold in the area. When we decided to call our book 'Gold from Norfolk', we knew that we should perhaps have called it 'Gold found in Norfolk'. As it has been under the soil on Ken Hill for over two thousand years, we thought that 'gold from Norfolk' was almost correct!

Those gold coins which were known to have come from Gaul could have been received by the Iceni as part payment for their trade with the Celtic tribes of Gaul. They give us a clue as to one possible origin of the Snettisham gold. The Celtic world covered much of Europe as we now know it. The Iceni metal-workers must have been paid in gold coin received from other Celtic tribes from their trading activity, perhaps by selling horses or corn to other tribes.

Their world was part of a network of trading links which stretched right across Europe and even down into the Mediterranean area. Gold coins could have come from Cornwall, where Celtic people had produced copper and tin to make bronze from an early date. There is a tradition in the tin mining areas of West Cornwall that tin was traded with the Phoenicians who could have traded for tin with gold. Or the Iceni gold could have come from Wales, where gold is still found today. Welsh gold was used for the wedding rings of Prince William and Kate.

But since these two gold Celtic coins were found on Ken Hill, the most likely source of some of the Snettisham gold was Gaul, what is now known as France, where Celtic tribes are known to have mined for gold in what is now the Limousin region and to have traded with the Iceni.

The name, Limousin, and the city of Limoges, both come from the name of the Celtic Tribe, the *Lemovices*. They occupied the Eastern edges of the Massive Central between 700 and 400 BC.

Limousin region in Central France (Gaul) by Jessie W.

Archaeologists now know that these Celtic people had at least 2,000 small open-cast gold mines in this region of Gaul before the Roman Conquest. They also panned for alluvial gold, fragments of gold in the gravel of river beds.

There is a vein, a narrow band of gold-bearing quartz, which runs east-west just to the north of the boundaries of the modern Dordogne and Haute-Vienne regions in the valleys around the villages of Jumilhac-le-Grand and St Yrieix-le-Perche.

In the museum of gold-mining in Jumilhac, there is a map showing a chain of these Celtic mining sites which runs along this band and which have been investigated by archeologists over the last thirty years.

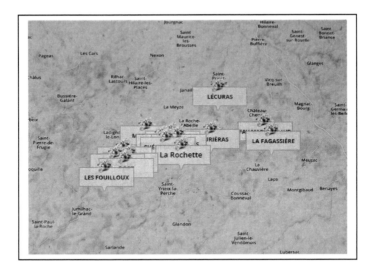

Fifteen of the known sites for Celtic gold mines in the Jumilhac area of the Limousin in France

Chateau of Jumilhac-le-Grand from the River Isle running through the wooded gorge below

In Jumilhac, you can book a day of searching for gold in the river bed using the method of 'panning'. River gravel is washed in a wide metal bowl until the tiny particles of the heavy gold are concentrated in the bottom. This is the classic way of getting gold from what are called 'alluvial' deposits of gravel, the way that gold was taken from the river beds of California and Australia and in the Canadian Klondike at the start of the gold-rush in each of these areas

Model of Celtic open-cast gold mining in Jumilhac museum

In the south of the Limousin, the band of gold-bearing quartz ran close to the surface and the *Lemovices* could dig it out from shallow open-caste pits and adits. By wedging tree-trunks across their diggings, they could climb up and down and pass the buckets of gold-bearing quartz up to the surface for processing.

The gold bearing quartz was first crushed with hammers and the powdered quartz was then roasted with charcoal. This made the small scraps of gold melt and run together into a bead of molten metal which formed in the bottom of the roasting dish. From this gold, the *Lemovices* could make the gold coins which they used for trading with other Celtic tribes right across Europe. One of these coins, showing the head of a Lemovice Chief, is shown below in this drawing by Jasmine D.

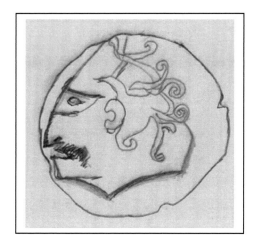

The *Lemovices'* gold contained about 20% silver, roughly the same proportion as that used in the Snettisham torcs and it is possible that gold from Jumilhac-le-Grand found its way to Ken Hill, Snettisham, where the Iceni used it to make their gold torcs.

When the Romans conquered this part of Gaul, the production of gold by the Celtics tribe for their own use ceased. All gold came under the control of the Romans when they enslaved the Gallic tribes. Gold production using Celtic slave labour will have continued for a time until the Romans found more convenient sources for their gold coinage from other parts of their vaste Empire.

8. Gold in today's world

Wherever the Iceni got their gold from, it was not pure gold which is very soft, but an alloy, a mixture of gold and silver called 'electrum'. Other metals are used today to make gold alloys which can be different colours, useful for making jewelry.

Coloured Gold

Yellow gold is made by mixing pure gold with silver and zinc, which also makes the gold more hard wearing. White gold is also more durable than yellow gold and can be made by alloying gold with platinum and nickel. Rose gold which has a pinkish colour is made when gold is alloyed with copper and silver. If just copper is used, you can make red gold. You can even make green gold by mixing it with silver, copper and a metal called cadmium, but this is poisonous!   *(by Jack W.)*

What is gold used for today?

There is an amazing variety of uses for gold, which fall under these headings: Aerospace, Awards, Dentistry, Electronics and Computers, Finance, Gilding, Glass, Medical, and of course Jewelry:

Aerospace: one interesting use of gold in Space is as a lubricant in places where oils cannot be used; because gold can form thin layers which slide over each other, it can be used to coat metal parts which have to rub against each other in space.

Awards: gold medals are awarded for success at the Olympics and World sporting events.

Dentistry: gold does not rust and is used to fill teeth as it is easy to work, is not poisonous and looks good!

Electronics and computing including mobile 'phones: gold is used in many places in desktop or laptop computers, as it is such a good conductor and does not corrode; nearly one billion mobile phones are produced world-wide each year and most of them contain about 30p worth of gold. Their average lifetime is under two years and very few are currently recycled. Although the amount of gold is small in each phone, the huge number means that a lot of gold is lost each year if the 'phones are not recycled.

Finance: it is still possible to buy gold sovereigns made by the Royal Mint to give to a child as an 'everlasting' gift; gold bullion is also held by some countries to provide a stable financial investment.

Glass: very small amounts of gold form tiny particles which can be scattered in glass to make the glass coloured, most commonly red.

Gilding: gold forms very thin layers called gold leaf and this is used to 'gild' many things, from cars to whole buildings! Very expensive china-ware is often decorated with gold, but this should not be put into washing-up machines as the chemicals used in washing damage the decoration!

Limoges porcelain decorated with gold leaf

Medical*: gold can be used as a drug to treat a small number of medical conditions and also it can be used as radioactive gold to help to treat some cancers*

*and the most important use from the earliest times to today is **Jewelry****: pure gold is too soft to stand up to the stresses which apply to many items of jewelry so it is often used in a mixture with silver to make it stronger.*

(by Sonny D. and Rowan D.)

Gold brooch made by the *Lemovices* in Gaul about 150 BC showing typical Celtic designs

The Iceni were not the only Celtic tribe to make gold torcs, they were made and worn by Celtic people right across the Celtic lands, including the Lemovices and other Gallic tribes.

What is the 'carat' system for gold and why is it important?

When you buy a gold wedding ring or a piece of gold jewelry, you want to know that you are getting good value for your money. But gold looks much the same, whether it is pure gold, the most valuable, or a mixture of gold and the cheaper metals, silver or copper. Jewellers can get their goods stamped with a 'hallmark' which tells you how much gold the piece contains and also where it was made and when

Suppose a jeweller offers a gold item for sale and the purchaser sees a set of marks stamped onto the item. Every gold item even today should have four hallmarks. One showing where it was assayed or checked for the purity of the gold, either in London (leopard's head), Birmingham (anchor), Sheffield (Yorkshire rose) or Edinburgh (castle). Our example has a leopard's head so was stamped in London.

Hallmarks on a gold object by Jasmine D.

The letter 'a' tells us about the date of the object. A small 'a' of this shape can be looked up in books where we find that it is the letter for the year 1721. So this gold object must be nearly three hundred years old.

Drawing and explanation by Callum E.

The third and fourth items are a number and a crown. In our case the number is 18, meaning that the gold is 18 carat or 18 parts of gold in 24 parts of metal. This is the system in the United Kingdom. In other parts of the world, the purity is expressed as a % or a decimal, so in this case it would be '75% or '0.75'or three parts of gold to one part of silver. 9 carat gold is the hardest gold and least pure of the types of gold used for jewelry. It is used for hard wearing items like wedding rings. 24 carat is pure gold, the most expensive but also the softest.

The crown symbol tells us that the item was assayed or tested for purity in England. If the mark is a thistle, that refers to Scotland. On some items, there is also a maker's stamp. In this case the letters A.N showing that the piece was made by a jeweller or goldsmith using this stamp – as yet unidentified!

The gold torcs which were found on Ken Hill were made over a thousand years before anyone thought of the system of hallmarks to guarantee purity. The Iceni had to take the quality of the gold that they found in coins or in torcs on trust and use it to make the items they wanted to wear or to give to their kings and queens.

Later on, men used the fact that pure gold and pure silver is relatively soft to try to decide whether it was genuine or not. That is why men in the Wild West of America would bite coins, gold or silver, to check precious metal rather than hard bronze or nickel. Another way of checking was to use strong acid, as gold is not attacked by acid whereas nickel and iron are dissolved.

But where does gold come from?

If the Snettisham gold torcs were made from gold coins traded by the Iceni from other areas, we wondered where the element gold came from in the first place. Did gold come from outer space like the iron which hits the earth as meteorites or was it in the earth from the beginning.

How gold is formed

There is a clue in the fact that gold can be made from other elements in the extreme conditions inside a nuclear reactor. This suggests that gold is formed in outer space in massive neutron stars by a process of supernova nucleosynthesis. When two of these huge stars collide, gold comes out of them. This gold is then delivered to the surface of the earth in or on asteroids. When the earth was first made, it was all molten and the gold would sink to the core of the planet. From there it could return to the surface by volcanic activity. Most of the gold today is thought to be in the earth's crust and mantle.

(by Oscar W.)

We also wondered how much gold there was in the world and how much had already been discovered.

How Much Gold is there?

Scientists think that there is enough gold and other precious metals in the core of the earth to cover the entire surface of the planet with a layer four metres thick. But according to the best estimate, all of the gold ever mined in the history of humanity, amounts to about 152,000 metric tons. This sounds a lot but it is actually only enough to fill 60 trailers or enough to cover Wimbledon Centre Court with gold 10m thick. Scientists believe that there is still eight times more gold dissolved in the waters of the oceans but the concentration of gold is so low it would be impossible to get it all out.

(by Jasmine D.)

9. Royal Norfolk

Boudica was Queen of the Iceni, the Iron Age Celtic people who occupied much of what is now Norfolk. But Boudica was not the only royal individual who has lived in the County of Norfolk.

Not far south of Snettisham is Sandringham House. Queen Victoria bought Sandringham in 1862 as a country home for her son, Albert Edward Prince of Wales, when he was 21. Sadly his father, Prince Albert died before the property was in Royal hands but the purchase went ahead and the Prince of Wales moved in with his wife, Princess Alexandra of Denmark. Subsequently, that house was demolished and then rebuilt in 1870. It has been used as a country home for the reigning Monarch and the Royal family ever since

Queen Victoria, the first Royal owner of Sandringham House

Her Majesty the Queen still uses Sandringham House as one of her Royal residences, her 'country retreat', and traditionally spends Christmas here with the Royal family and their guests.

Sandringham House from the front lawns

Prince William and Kate and their children live in their own home at Anmer Hall on the Sandringham Estate, not far from our village of Snettisham.

There are many 'royal' organisations in Norfolk, such as the Royal Norfolk Show and the Royal West Norfolk Golf Club.

Some places are called 'royal' including counties, boroughs, towns and even parishes. For example, Berkshire is a Royal County because the Queen has a palace at Windsor. The County was granted Royal status by the Queen in 1957. Greenwich was made a Royal Borough by the Queen to mark the Millennium in 2000, Kingston on Thames was granted the status because it was the birthplace of the Anglo-Saxon King Aethelstan in 924. He became the first King of the English. George V granted them the status of Royal Borough because it had been recognised as Royal 'from time immemorial'.

The parish of Wootton Basset became Royal Wootton Basset in recognition of their response to the repatriation of military personnel at the nearby RAF base. In Scotland, the area around the Queen's Scottish home at Balmoral is officially called 'Royal Deeside'.

But when you drive into the County of Norfolk today, you will pass a sign which proclaims Norfolk to be 'Nelson's County'. Which is true, but why not 'Royal Norfolk'?

There was an attempt to change this by sending a petition signed by very many people to the Houses of Parliament. But it failed, as the notice on the next page states. Since our book is a celebration of Norfolk, the Iceni Queen Boudica and gold, perhaps we should send a copy to Her Majesty with the respectful request that she does grant the County of Norfolk Royal Status in recognition of the link with the Queen of the North Folk, the Iceni people, who lived in Norfolk long before Anglo-Saxon King Aethelstan was born in Kingston on Thames.

Make Norfolk a Royal County

With the Queen and two future Kings residing in Norfolk, it should receive Royal County Status. Past Sovereigns have also passed away in the County and Diana Princess of Wales also grew up in Norfolk.

This petition was rejected

Why was this petition rejected? It's about something that the UK Government or Parliament is not responsible for.

The title 'Royal' is a privilege granted by the Queen. This action could not, therefore, be taken directly by the Government or Parliament.

You could start a petition calling on the Government to recommend to Her Majesty that she grant the title "Royal" to the county of Norfolk.

We only reject petitions that don't meet the petition standards.

Timeline of Periods of Our History

4500-2000 BC   Neolithic (New Stone Age)

2000-700   BC   Bronze Age (the period of Grimes Graves flint mines)

700 BC–43 AD   Iron Age (the pre-Roman period of Iceni occupation of Norfolk)

43 – 410 AD   Roman (including Boudica's time)

440 - 1066 AD   Saxon Kingdoms (up to the Battle of Hastings)

793 – 1066 AD   Vikings (who moved into and occupied the East and North of England)

1066 – 1485 AD   Norman and Medieval

1485 – 1603 AD   Tudors

1603 – 1714 AD   Stuarts

1714 – 1837 AD   Georgian

1837 – 1901 AD   Victorian

Sources

We used the following sources to research this book:

Bond, Richard**, Penn,** Kenneth and **Rogerson,** Andrew '*4: The North Folk; Angles, Saxons and Danes*' in the Norfolk Origins series Poppyland Publishing 1990

Cauuet, Béatrice, *'L'or des Celtes du Limousin'* Culture et Patrimoine en Limousin 2004

Davies, John *'The Land of Boudica – Prehistoric and Roman Norfolk'* Norfolk Museums and Archaeology Service 2008

Davies, John and **Robinson**, Bruce *'Boudica – Her Life, Times and Legacy'* Poppy Publishing 2009

Dio, Cassius *'The Roman History'* 155-235 AD adapted from the translation on the website:
penelope.uchicago.edu/Thayer/E/Roman/Texts/Cassius_Dio

Farley, Jane and **Hunter**, Fraser *'Celts – Art and History'* The British Museum 2015

Murray, Peter *'The Parish Church of St Mary's, Snettisham'* Diocese of Norwich 2013

Prior, Francis *'Flag Fen – life and death of a prehistoric landscape'* The History Press 2005

Tacitus *'The Annals'* written 109 AD, translated by Alfred John Church and William Jackson Brodribb and adapted for current use, from the classics.mit.edu/Tacitus/annals.html website

The **Guide to Norwich Museum**

The Poster on **the Snettisham Hoard** and text, from the Castle Museum, Norwich

The Poster on **Venta Icenorum** and text, from the Castle Museum, Norwich

Vivacity 'Exploring Roman Peterborough –guided walks through history

and the many web-sites consulted without supervision by the Pupils of Birch Class.

Thanks

Many individuals have helped us with this books and we would like to thank them all:

At Snettisham Primary School, Norfolk

Mrs C Holmes, Class Teacher, Mr L Enters, Class Teacher, Mrs V Rose, Secretary, Mrs Holland, High Level Teaching Assistant, Mrs Scott, Learning Support Assistant, Mr L Stevens (former Headteacher), Mrs N Darley, Headteacher, and all the Pupils of Birch Class. 2015-2016 and 2016-2017

At Barny Books – our Publishers

Mrs Molly Burkett and Mrs Jayne Thompson

At Spiegl Press, Stamford – our Printers

Mr Hugo Spiegl

And Julian Bower Associates Ltd – our Sponsors

And Mrs Jenny Haden, for her support and for putting up with all the visits to Norfolk and time spent writing, editing and managing for this book project when there were other jobs to be done